SHORT SETTER'S HANDBOOK

LINDSEY BERG

THEARTOFCOACHINGVOLLEYBALL.COM

Printed in the United States of America

First Printing, 2019

ISBN: 978-0-9989765-9-4

Written by Lindsey Napela Berg
Edited by Don Patterson
Instructional photos by Peter Brouillet
Cover photo by Don Liebig

Published by Total Sports, LLC
3720 SW 141st Avenue, Suite 209
Beaverton, OR 97005

www.theartofcoachingvolleyball.com

For my mom and dad, who believed in me from day one, my grandmother, who inspires me with her can-do attitude and enthusiasm for life, and my sister, who is undoubtedly my rock.

TABLE OF CONTENTS

FOREWARD

Is it possible for this proud father to objectively evaluate the level of talent of his daughter's volleyball ability? After all, as a player and coach, I should be able to put aside any prejudice or favoritism. For daughter Lindsey, there was no need for anything other than watching her develop as an elite player through her own relentless efforts to learn and improve her skills.

Before turning 10 years old, she persuaded anyone and everyone to pepper with her. If no one was available, she would set the ball against walls, including ones inside our home. At 10, she graduated to "baby court" games at the Outrigger Canoe Club and eventually to junior club competition where she discovered her exceptional will to win and the unbearable disappointment of losing.

She had an all-around game after playing beach doubles at the Outrigger. Setting was her specialty, but with an efficiently powerful arm swing, she succeeded as a hitter and developed a lethal jump serve. In juniors and college competition, she became one of the early pioneers of that skill in the girls' and women's game. Points won from her jump serving were consistently a determining factor in many wins. Most noteworthy was leading the Big Ten in aces all four years she played for the University of Minnesota. That was, and still is, a rare accomplishment.

More valuable, however, were her mental toughness and leadership skills as an elite setter. Coaches at all levels have been impressed with her high volleyball IQ, recognizing her successful playmaking as a direct result of her instincts for reading the defense. She was the ultimate quarterback who could get the most out of every hitter, letting them know she would set them in the right place at the right time.

Lindsey at the World Cup in 2011 with her grandmother, Gertrude Berger, her mom, Tina, and her dad, Dennis. PHOTO: FIVB

Lindsey's 8th grade teammate told her, in no uncertain terms, that she would play in the Olympics. Fast forward 10 years and Lindsey was doing just that – representing the U.S. at the 2004 Athens Olympic Games. Not sure if the psychic teammate knew how many hurdles Lindsey needed to get over to do so, but with passion, determination and a positive attitude, she overcame prejudices and rejection for being too short and not having the right athletic body type. Lindsey's continued pursuit of excellence led her to become a three-time Olympian with two silver medals (2008 and 2012).

Lindsey identifies "cuore" as a main ingredient in her success. It means "heart" in Italian. Her heart is always filled with an intense desire to practice and improve, to relentlessly compete for a victory, to get along with teammates and lead them in a direction that will accomplish that victory.

As her father, I am most proud of how Lindsey sets such a great example for athletes who, in the eyes of others, are underestimated and not supposed to achieve a high level of success. With a burning desire, a strong mindset and self-confidence, she "set" a standard for herself to reach and perform to the best of her ability at every level of competition. It can happen, did happen and will happen, even for the short setter!

— **Dennis Berg**, Lindsey's dad

Chapter 1

ISLAND GIRL

I've played volleyball ever since I can remember. Growing up in Honolulu, a place where the sport is celebrated, made it very easy to love volleyball. Being on the beach volleyball courts at the Outrigger Canoe Club every weekend made it very easy to love volleyball. Being surrounded consistently by volleyball greats made it easy to love volleyball. And having a supportive dad who was also a player and coach made it easy to love volleyball.

For those of you who don't know me well or at all, you will now. My name is Lindsey Napela Berg. I was born and raised in Hawaii. My parents, Tina and Dennis Berg, are a big reason for my success in the sport, and the support of the rest of my family was a big factor, too. My sister, Erin Lindsey, my grandmother,

Gertrude Berger, and many others in my incredible family were there for me throughout a journey that I never could have imagined.

My father played at UC Santa Barbara, then coached some of the greatest coaches of the recent past and played with some of the best volleyball players in the world. Fortunately, he began coaching me at a young age when I was vertically challenged. I was the ball/water girl when he coached at Iolani, a high school in Honolulu. When he began teaching and coaching at Punahou School, which is noted for its great volleyball tradition and has produced players such as Stein Metzger, Kevin and Scott Wong, and Mike and Debbie Lambert, I considered myself the assistant coach at age 10. I would pepper every time I could talk one of the players into it, and I did some damage to my parents' house practicing my setting against the wall and working on my arm swing. I always wanted to be a hitter. I would beg my dad to open the gym so I could jump serve 100 balls. It was nonstop, and it wasn't because Dad pushed me. It was me. I loved the game, and I wanted to practice and get really good.

I played intermediate in the 7th and 8th grade for my dad and then made varsity at Punahou in 9th grade. That year I got to play with my sister. Erin was also a setter, so I got to be a hitter. It was quite entertaining. Throughout those years, I played club volleyball for what was then known as ASICS Rainbows. Run through after run through, my coaches, Dave Shoji, then the head coach of the Hawaii women's team, and Charlie Wade, who is now head coach of the Hawaii men's team, would tell me to run faster, get lower, jump higher and basically do everything better than I was doing it.

As I approached my junior year, the recruiting process started, which was much later than it is now. (In today's game, as you probably know, kids are actually signing with colleges before they even start high school.) Coaches who had never seen me play but only read that I was a certain height and weight would not even give me a look. No doubt I was the best setter in my class, but coaches were worried about all kinds of things. Was I tall enough at barely 5-8? Was I fast enough? Was I skinny enough? Could I jump high enough to touch the ball when blocking? Could I play at the highest level? It was so hurtful. I didn't understand it. I could run a team, lead a team, and do everything like no other. Not to mention, I cared. And I had heart and passion.

Through a grueling recruiting process of being either turned down or not wanting to commit before I saw the school so they took the next choice, I ended up at the University of Minnesota with Mike Hebert. He believed in me and wanted me to build his program with him.

Hawaii to Minnesota was definitely a shocker, and to this day I have a hard time answering the question of how it happened. Now it's all a little blurry, but what I do know is I would not be the volleyball player or person I am today if I didn't challenge myself and follow through with the challenge.

Minnesota was cold – very cold. And we were awful my first year, losing 9 of our final 12 matches. I wanted to transfer, but I stuck it out and I'm glad I did.

Throughout my college career I was criticized for everything all over again. Fat, short, slow, can't block. Blah, blah, blah. Building the Minnesota team, taking them to the Elite 8, breaking school and Big Ten records, never being an All-American. That's when the chip on my shoulder developed. It pissed me off, to say the least.

In 2002, timing led me to play in the only year of the United States Professional Volleyball League (USPV). I was drafted by the Minnesota Chill, and we ended up upsetting the stacked Chicago Thunder to win the championship. My assistant coach was Kevin Hambly, who later became the head coach at Illinois and is currently the head women's coach at Stanford. He was responsible for talking Toshi Yoshida, then the head USA women's coach, into allowing me to try out for the national team since – shocker – I had never been asked before. I was told I had to pay my own travel expenses to Colorado Springs for a two-week tryout. If I made it past the two weeks, they said they would reimburse me.

My dad and I packed up my car from Minnesota and headed to Colorado Springs. The training sessions were torture. We had 8-hour days. The first week, I could barely walk or even sit on the toilet. (I was chugging gallons of water to stay hydrated, which didn't help.) Multiple times I thought about packing my bags and leaving. Thankfully, my training teammates wouldn't let me.

Slowly but surely I made it through three weeks, and one by one I was beating out the other setters that had either been there for a while or arrived when I did. I became the starting setter while Robyn Ah-Mow had her baby and was getting back in shape. When it came close to the 2004 Athens Olympics, I was named to the team. I remember the meeting very clearly. I was confident I would make it. I knew how hard I had worked. I knew that I had made other people better. I knew they had to take me.

I remember Kevin laughing at me afterward, saying something like, "You didn't even seem excited or surprised." I said, "I wasn't surprised, and my face rarely shows excitement." Ha! I had beaten all odds. "Short, fat, slow" girl from Hawaii, never an All-American, was going to the Olympics.

When we got to Athens, I did show excitement. How could you not? My friends and family were so proud of me and excited as well, which is priceless. I remember the day someone told me to go on Volleytalk because people were saying great things about me making the team. So I did. Well, along with a couple of praises were hundreds of disbeliefs. People couldn't believe I made it. It was back to: "She is short. She is fat. She isn't an All-American. The other setters should have made it." There I was at my first Olympics after leaving blood, sweat and tears in Colorado Springs to make it and I was crying my eyes out. I couldn't believe people still felt this way about me. But like I always do, I sucked it up. I was the back-up, and I went in every match as a double-sub and did all I could for the team.

Unfortunately, we didn't reach our potential, and it was a very disappointing Olympics. We finished fifth. But I knew I deserved to be there, and I also knew I had represented my country well.

With the disappointment of the Olympics, I lost some love for the game. I wasn't having fun anymore, and I was contemplating quitting. I had never been a quitter, but I had such a bad taste in my mouth.

Luckily, an Italian coach, Marcello Abbondanza, and his team, Scavolini Pesaro, came to the rescue, offering me a contract that I couldn't turn down. The thought of getting my first love back gave me hope. There I went, off to another challenge.

I spent three years in Italy playing for Pesaro, there again hearing people speak of what I was and what I wasn't. But my play spoke louder, my leadership was undeniable, and I flat out just made people better. And what I wanted to happen happened. I loved volleyball again. And I knew I wanted to try for another Olympics since the first one didn't go so well. I was determined to do what no one thought I could do.

Fast forward to Beijing in 2008, when I made the Olympic team again, played my heart out and helped the U.S. win a silver medal. People still couldn't believe I was on the team. Now it was getting humorous. Not even two Olympics and four seasons in Italy in what was the best league in the world at that time could shut people up.

Setting the U.S. to a silver medal in 2012 at the London Olympics.

After Beijing, I took a season off and had knee surgery. But I wasn't ready to be done. I wanted to go again. I wanted gold. I wanted to start every match. I wanted to make people better. I wanted to become a professional leader.

I played three more seasons in Italy with an amazing team and made the London Olympics, my third. Guess what?

People still were talking trash about me. I played the best volleyball of my life and had the time of my life. Unfortunately, we came up a little short of gold, taking the silver once again. But I had zero regrets. I left it all out there on the court.

My knee was bothering me again after the Olympics, and I wanted to take a little time off. But I was addicted. I don't know if I was addicted to playing, proving people wrong or what it was, but I wanted another one. I didn't want to leave the game while I was playing my best, even though I realize now that it would have been a good idea. I ended up playing one more professional season, then mutually deciding with the national team coach at the time, Karch Kiraly, that it was time to be finished. My knee had become such an issue that it seemed like playing three more years to get to Rio in 2016 wouldn't have been good for my long-term health.

Moral of the story is, I dealt with criticism and doubts my whole career and overcame them. Initially, it came from coaches who didn't know me very well or even ones who did know me. It was constant – coaches wishing I was taller, wishing I was faster, wishing I was skinnier.

I think there was a stereotypical volleyball type when I was growing up. Women were always lean and thin. It has changed, in my opinion. You need to be a lot stronger as a women's volleyball player to compete with the great athletes out there, not just a tall, lean stick. But I still think there are stereotypes that the shorter volleyball player or the thicker volleyball player or maybe the more skilled but not as athletic volleyball player has to deal with. It's very complicated trying to keep up with what society thinks looks good or is athletic, so my advice to you is this: Don't try. Just work to be your best.

With that in mind, I've written this book. It's meant to speak to all volleyball players who, at some point or another, have felt they were overlooked or undervalued because of their height, weight or athleticism. My hope is that you'll use it to do what I did in my career: prove 'em wrong.

Chapter 2

PLAYING WITH A CHIP ON YOUR SHOULDER

When you grow up being a shorter player in the sport of volleyball, you know that you're always going to have to do a little more than the taller players. You have to know the game better, work harder, train harder, figure out different tricks that can give you an advantage. The chip on your shoulder helps. You are out there to prove everyone wrong.

The first thing you have to do is develop a mentality that height doesn't matter. What does matter are:

- Skills
- Knowledge of the game, your teammates and your opponents
- Leadership qualities
- Ability to make those around you better

It's extremely important that you never give up, no matter what coaches, peers or anyone tell you. I never knew I would be an Olympian, but I did know that I loved the game, knew how to work hard and hated losing. All of those things kept me going during the tough times.

I remember when I was playing in the 14 and under age group. After JO's and The Volleyball Festival (in my day, we could play in both of those tournaments), my teammates and I tried out for the Jr. National Team. I had the best tryout ever. I won all the competitions, got along well with everyone and felt that I had proved my skill and worth. I left feeling very excited about my chances to make the team or at least to be invited to a tryout for the team. A couple of weeks later, I was notified that neither I nor my teammates had made it. I was pissed, to say the least. But I didn't let it stop me. And that is when the chip on my shoulder developed. From then on, I practiced and played at another level. It was time to prove myself to the volleyball world.

If you're a smaller setter, you'll never be denied a position on the court if you are a leader and make the other players around you better. As you work on your setting, work on your communication just as much. Work on how to talk to your teammates. Take responsibility and make your hitters better. Even when it's not your fault or you don't think it is, focus on how you can fix it, not on assessing blame. Talk to your hitters all the time. Talk to your passers all the time. Work on having a good relationship with your coach. All of these things will make it not matter that you are a smaller setter.

With that said, let's talk specifics:

IMPROVING YOUR SKILLS

Obviously, there are many, many skills that setters need to have, and my goal here is not to give you a comprehensive list of every one of them. Instead, I'd like to cover some of the skills that you have the ability to work on by yourself.

- **Hands** — You can never touch the ball too much. Get to know the feeling of the ball and have full control over it. That can be accomplished by just holding the ball often, feeling the ball and becoming one with the ball. Lie down and set the ball straight up. Set against the wall. Move your hand position and figure

Lying on the floor and setting straight up is a good way to develop touch.

out what is best for you to have the most control over the ball. Hands, hands, hands.

- **Footwork** — In my world, there isn't just one way to get to the ball. There are many. Different players are better at certain types of footwork. The key is to get to the ball as fast as you can, so you should practice all different types of footwork. Run, skip, crossover, shuffle, jump, you name it. By working on all of them, you can be ready for every situation.
- **Serving**—Master your serve. I was known for my jump serve. I would go to the gym and serve 100 balls or more growing up. Serving is one thing that you have full control over, like a basketball free throw.

My jump serve was a big weapon for me in college and on the national team. PHOTO: DON LIEBIG

Height doesn't matter for these skills. Practice matters. Hard work matters. Determination to be the best matters. Which leads to another topic that can make you the best ...

KNOWING THE GAME

Most players, especially those who reach the college level, understand the basics of volleyball, but a setter needs to know everything about the game. And when I say you need to know the game better than those around you, I'm talking specifically about things like:

- Where your teammates are supposed to be. You have to know exactly where each player should be lined up no matter what rotation you're in. This is part of your job.
- What plays in certain situations are best to call and why. For example, if your opponent has a short setter blocking, you'll probably want to run plays that keep the other team's middle on your middle and then send the ball to the outside over the short setter.
- How does your opponent play? What are their tendencies? Watch video or watch teams during breaks at tournaments. Pay attention to what your coach tells you about the other team. If the other team sets the middle a lot, you need to know that. Or maybe their defense starts way back in the court. The more specifics you know, the better you'll run the offense.

Have you ever thought about how many points are lost during the course of a season because someone on your team didn't know that the opposing setter was in the front row? It's the setter's job to make sure that doesn't happen. It's the setter's responsibility to know everything. Sounds tough, and it is. That's why exceptional setters are hard to come by. But the best ones know the game like no other and become the best leaders, which brings me to the next topic.

LEADERSHIP

Dating all the way back to middle school, I was known as a leader. I was the best on the team. I was passionate. And I voiced it. Isn't that what a leader is? You can definitely start there. That's a good base. But the best leaders work on improving their leadership skills just as much as they work on improving their physical and playing skills.

I'd say I really began to understand this when I was a freshman at the University of Minnesota. There was an older setter starting ahead of me when I arrived. I was prepared for that, but I knew I had to go above and beyond to make sure I was on the court. At first, I didn't want to step on any toes because I was the newcomer, but that only lasted about a week. The team had leaders, including the type of leader I mentioned above. But they didn't have this leader.

I began to talk to everyone more and get to know them better. You want to ask questions to players and coaches. Take everything in. Ask specifics. What kinds of sets do each of your teammates want? Take responsibility if you don't provide exactly what they want. When I could, I would stay late after practice. I would demand the most from myself. That is what a leader does. I got better and better at communicating, understanding my teammates and, at the end of the day, making everyone around me better, which is the last skill I want to emphasize.

Developing a close bond with your teammates translates to better play on the court.
PHOTO: FIVB

MAKE YOUR TEAMMATES BETTER

As I said earlier, a coach can't leave you on the bench if you make your teammates better. As you become a better leader, the skills associated with that will make your teammates better. If you communicate with them consistently about the set they desire, or talk after the play about how to make it better, you are making your teammates better. If you learn how to communicate with each person on your team – and remember, each one will communicate differently and respond differently – you will then learn how to bring out the best in them. Whether it's asking them to do something, or just flat-out cheering for them and motivating them, all of this makes them better.

I always found that taking responsibility earns the trust of your teammates. When you have their trust, the whole team works better together. And the great thing about it is it's contagious. Once the goal of making each other better is clear, it is very easy to get everyone to buy into it.

Chapter 3

CONNECTING WITH THE MIDDLE

Connecting with a middle attacker is one of the harder skills to perfect in volleyball. For the setter to put the ball in the right place every time with ease, the timing of the middle attacker needs to be consistent. Unfortunately, it's not realistic that middle attackers are going to be consistent with their timing and location.

If the pass is perfect, one could say that it's easier for a taller setter to connect with a middle attacker since they will be at a similar height when the setter releases the ball to the hitter. But passes are rarely perfect, so height isn't really a factor if the setter is good at the following:

- Seeing their middle hitter.

- Understanding if their middle hitter is on time.
- Knowing if their middle hitter is in the right place.
- Knowing what the blocker on the other side of the net is doing.

To do all of this well, you don't need to be tall. You just need good vision, good technique and quick feet. Here are four things to work on:

1. Reading the pass. As a setter, you can get a head start on knowing where the pass is going to end up by reading the passer's platform. First, get your eyes on the passer as quickly as possible and make sure you are facing where the ball is coming from.

If the shoulders are back (left), the pass will likely be off the net. If the shoulders are pointed toward the net (right), the ball will likely be closer to the net.

Watching the passer's shoulders and the platform contact on the ball can allow you to anticipate the direction and trajectory of the pass. If shoulders are back and the platform is under the ball, the ball will likely go up and off the net. Conversely, if a passer's shoulders are pointing toward the net and the platform is on the back of the ball, the pass will be a flatter trajectory and closer to the net. From the setter position, the more you can watch your teammates pass, the better you will get at anticipating where the ball will go.

2. Quick footwork. If you can get to the ball quickly, you'll have more opportunities to set your middle attacker, even if the pass is on the 10-foot line. Try all different kinds of footwork: two legs, one leg, jump set, on the ground, etc. Be creative.

3. Keeping your hands high (above your forehead) in most situations. It's important to maintain a neutral setting position where you can set both forward or backward without having to make significant adjustments with your body to get the ball where you want it. This also makes it harder for the opposing blocker to read where you are likely to set. As I got better and better, I sometimes dropped my hands to deceive blockers as well. As

you get better, you may want to do this too. Lower hands make it harder for the opposing middle. When you drop your hands to set, you are ultimately waiting longer to set the ball, which may make the blocker wait to move or read. That often makes the blocker late to block your hitter. Changing the timing of when you set the ball (high, neutral, low) keeps the blocker unsure about when you will deliver the ball and therefore makes it more difficult for them to read and time their jump.

High hands allow you to set forward or backward.

Good hand contact with the ball gives you more control.

4. Having strong, fast wrists. Getting the ball out of your hands quickly is very important if the middle attacker is on time. If the middle attacker isn't on time, work to a level where you're able to hold the ball a little longer to wait for your middle attacker. A good way to practice this is to start by catching the ball, making sure to have as many fingers around the ball as possible. The more contact with the ball, the more control and strength. Then toss to yourself and start to set the ball at different speeds with different tension or strength from your hands and wrists. An easy place to practice this on your own is against a wall.

Setting against a wall is a great way to practice on your own.

Chapter 4

WEAPONS FOR SMALL BLOCKERS

We were playing in the FIVB's Grand Prix tournament against Italy. I had competed against the Italians for many years and also alongside a few of them as teammates on foreign club teams. Throughout my professional career, the Italians always tried to go after me because they thought they could hit over me. It happened here and there, but often I would surprise them. My timing was always key to getting good touches. Since I was small, they couldn't really see me, and they would end up hitting down into me thinking I wasn't there.

In this match, we came from behind. The final game was extremely close. When we got to match point, I knew what was coming: They would set to the outside hitter, thinking she could hit over me, use me, or do whatever she wanted.

Well, they were wrong. I waited, waited and timed it perfectly. The set was tight. I pushed my hands over low and tight and blocked it back in the hitter's face.

For some reason, I still remember that match as clearly as if it happened yesterday. It wasn't the biggest game, but I almost surprised myself with my discipline in the things that really matter. Timing and hands. Not height and jumping ability.

And on plays when I didn't get a block or a touch, I stayed focused on one of the most important keys for short setters who want to be assets to their teams as blockers: "If they hit over you, so be it. Stay disciplined. Your defense can play around you."

Keep in mind, though, you won't have blocking success without developing the proper skills. Two of the most important are timing and hand-positioning.

TIMING

If your timing is correct, you'll get a similar number of blocks and touches as a taller setter. Promise!

In general, the key to good timing in blocking (especially as a shorter player) is to wait longer than you think you should. During my playing career at the University of Minnesota and on the U.S. national team, I would constantly tell myself, "Wait, wait, wait!" It takes some getting used to because your first instinct is to jump sooner. But you have to be disciplined about waiting until the hitter has already jumped.

The process of blocking starts with watching the pass, then watching the setter to determine where the ball is being set. Next, your eyes should go immediately to the hitter. Watch the approach. That will give you cues on where you should line up. Consider whether you are taking ball, angle or line. The height of the set is also a consideration. If the set is a slower, higher ball, wait even longer – longer than you would ever think. You are already at a disadvantage height-wise, so the worst thing you can do is jump early and be on your way down when the hitter hits the ball. If it's a fast ball, you will almost be chasing after the set.

DISCIPLINE THAT HELPS YOUR DEFENDERS

For smaller blockers, it's very important to be disciplined so the defense can dig around you. Know the game plan and what you are taking, and let your back row know. Even if you are not high over the net, a solid, stable block is very effective. A touch can be just as valuable to your team as a block back to the other side.

HAND POSITIONING

With your hands, your goal is to be low and tight. What I mean by this is you should have the least amount of space between your hands/arms and the net. Your block move should be one fluid motion. It's not up, then over. It's just directly over the net. If you try to go up first with the idea that it will help you get your hands higher, that split second could lead to more of a slapping motion and cause the timing of your hands to be off. That means more space between the net and your arms, which can lead to you being tooled.

Correct **Incorrect**

Penetrating over the net (left) rather than just putting your hands straight up (right) is key to effective blocking.

Making sure your hands are big is also important, especially for undersized blockers. You should feel the webbing between your fingers stretching so your fingers are spread wide and the surface area of your hands is as big as possible.

Forming a big surface area with your hands will help you block more balls.

SOFT BLOCKING

As much as it may seem like a disadvantage not to be able to get way up like the bigger girls, there are positives. When your arms are not as high, they're not as much of a target for the hitter to use.

One technique that has been used forever by shorter players is called "soft blocking." If you're a setter who can't get even one bit over the net, it's useful to learn how to soft block. Here are the two biggest differences between soft blocking and regular blocking:

1. The objective is NOT to get your hands over the net because you're not looking to send the ball back into your opponent's court but, rather, deflect it upward so your teammates can play it.
2. Your wrists go the other way, so your palms are facing up rather than angling downward toward the other side of the court. Again, this is about how you want the ball to deflect off your hands. The more it pops up on your side of the court, the easier it will be for your teammates to dig it and transition into a good offensive play.

To soft block, position your hands back so you can deflect the ball up.

SWING BLOCKING

Swing blocking is another technique that can benefit shorter blockers. The motion allows you to reach a higher point over the net. Why is that? Well, swing blocking is almost like an approach to hit, which gives you more momentum and a higher jump. Another reason is that it allows you to start inside to help with the quick attack, then get out to the pin more efficiently.

Coaches teach this skill differently, whether it's the footwork or the way you swing your arms. The footwork that I found most effective was:

- Big first right step
- Smaller left-right step, like a gather

Initially, your arms should be up in front of your face or even higher to help with the quick ball. Then, as you see that the set is going outside, keep your elbows and arms tight to your body as you do your footwork. Eventually, swing your arms low and tight over the net, trying to grab the ball on the other side.

You and your middle blocker should be in sync as you do your movement to the outside. It's important to practice this footwork and timing alone and with your middle blockers to feel comfortable. There will be times you feel out of control. Don't worry. You'll get the hang of it!

THE JOUST

Another skill you'll want to work on is the one- or two-handed joust. The main key here is to jump later than your opponent and touch the ball second. This gives you leverage to push the ball to the other side of the net. If you can push last, the ball will likely end up on your opponent's side rather than your side.

FINDING WHAT WORKS FOR YOU

Toward the end of my career, my coaches decided it was more important for me to get a good touch than to help with the middle attack, so sometimes I would swing block, other times I would already be on the outside covering that area.

It's important to learn and try these different types of blocking techniques. At the end of the day, your coach will determine what works best for you and the team, but being adaptable and having a good attitude about trying new techniques will serve you well.

It's worth pointing out that for four straight Olympics – 2000 (Sydney), 2004 (Athens), 2008 (Beijing) and 2012 (London) – our starting setter on the women's team was under 5-8. In Sydney and Beijing, the setter was Robyn Ah-Mow, who is 5-7. In Beijing, I was the setter along with Robyn. In London,

I was the starter and our other setter was Courtney Thompson, who is also 5-7. In both 2008 and 2012, we won silver medals.

I'm sure you get my point. If shorter than 5-8 works at the Olympic level, it will obviously work at every level. Wink!

Chapter 5

MOVING TO THE BALL

One thing that we all might agree on in the volleyball world is that there is a big possibility that a shorter/smaller setter will make faster moves to the ball. But that wouldn't be a good enough reason to choose a shorter setter over a taller setter because efficient footwork and reading can be taught to setters of all sizes. That being said, I do believe you can teach an already quick smaller setter to be more efficient and read even better, which is a huge positive for a team.

Just like there are different levels in volleyball overall, there are varying levels to footwork. When I was young and throughout college, I practiced my footwork over and over again. I did repetitions of each of the possible footwork patterns that might come up during a match, hoping at the end of the day that they would become so natural and ingrained that I wouldn't have to think about them. But even though I went through all of those reps, my theory now is "Just get to the ball." I don't care how you get there. Just get there as fast as you can.

I know you may be thinking, "Easy for you to say after playing in three Olympics." But I really think this "just get there" philosophy should apply to setters at all levels of volleyball. Some will be better at shuffling, others crossing over, still others might want to just simply run.

Since you're looking to me for advice, I will break down the different ways I learned and the ways I teach so you can experiment and decide what works best for you.

IMPROVING EFFICIENCY

To be efficient means achieving maximum productivity with minimum wasted effort or expense. It's one thing to say, "Get to the ball faster," but at the end of the day if you are efficient with your steps you will get there as fast as you can.

I'm going to talk about footwork options related to the location of the pass. I will also refer to rhythm and cover the left-right finishing footwork that I used as a player. Some coaches might teach the opposite, but I am here to teach what made me the setter I am. Rhythm and left-right finishing footwork were two very big keys for me.

PERFECT PASS ON THE NET

Setting is about rhythm. If the pass is perfect, you will use a left-right foot pattern under the ball (see photos below), unless you're jump setting and no movement is needed to get to the ball. In that case, you will only need to walk a couple of steps to the ball.

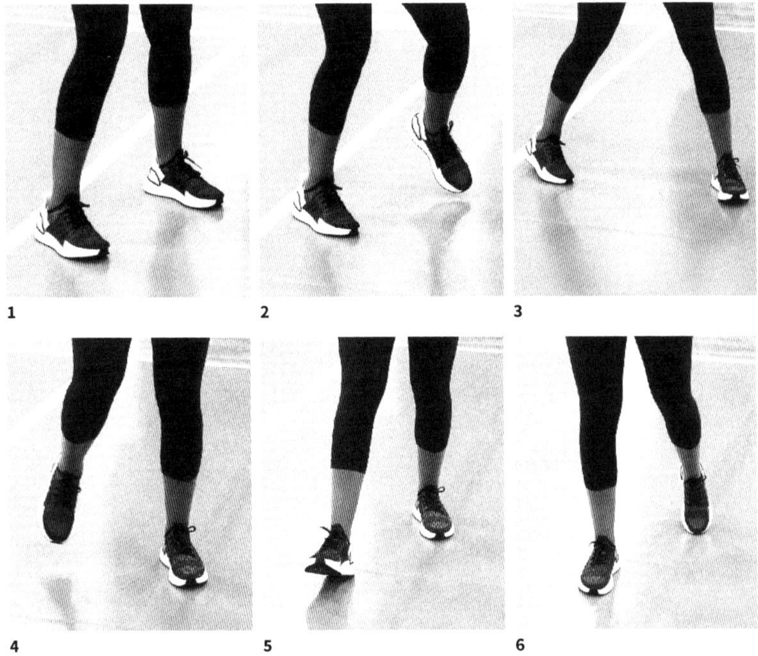

The left-right footwork pattern helps you establish a good setting rhythm. Start by stepping with your left foot. Turn toward Zone 4 if you're not already facing that direction, then push off with your back foot (left foot). Finally, take a step with your right foot and transfer your weight forward.

PASS A FEW FEET OFF THE NET

For passes that are close but not right on the net, you have several options:

1. **Shuffle, shuffle:** This is simple enough. You take a couple of shuffles toward the ball, then finish with your left-right footwork – or a jump, if you are jump-setting.

Shuffle, shuffle footwork is an efficient way to get your feet to the ball.

2. **Step, crossover:** Here, you take a step in the direction of the ball with your left foot, then follow with a crossover step with your right. Finish with your left-right footwork or a jump for the jump set.

Step, crossover footwork is another good way to get your feet to the ball. Once you turn toward your target (photos 5 and 6), finish by using the same footwork demonstrated on page 34 – pushing off with your left foot and stepping forward with your right.

3. **Step, crossover off one leg:** As with the "step, crossover," this starts with a step with your left foot in the direction of the ball. Next, take a crossover step that results in a one-legged jump off your right foot as you turn to square up to the target. This is a more advanced move.

Step, crossover off one leg is more advanced than the two-step movements.

PASS TO THE 10-FOOT LINE

Same technique as the other moves, except you will take an extra step and or shuffle.

FAR OUT-OF-SYSTEM PASS

If the pass is really bad, run as fast as you can to get your feet to the ball. This gives you the best chance to get square to the net. You may not be able to, but you definitely won't if you don't go full speed.

When the ball is this far off, you may have to bump set. A good way to gauge whether you have time to set the ball with your hands or go to the bump is whether the ball is above or below your chest. Above, use your hands. Below, use the bump.

Your best results in this situation will come if you can be fully stopped before you contact the ball with your platform, but this isn't always possible. But either way, your sets will be more consistent if you use your legs so you can get a down-up motion. That's something I learned from one of my coaches on the U.S. team, Toshi Yoshida, and it's a great tip for all setters.

Be sure to finish your platform motion where you want the ball to go. This is especially important on the plays where you don't have time to stop and have to run through the ball.

FAST PASS ONE STEP OFF THE NET

This is a little more advanced, but if a pass is coming to you low and a step off the net, you can take one step with your left as you pivot to face the target. This is a good trick to have in your repertoire.

The positives of being efficient to the ball are endless. Setters, like middle blockers, are constantly moving. It's always a plus to save energy when you can. It is inevitable that the setter will run around all game. But unnecessary steps prevent you from saving energy, which could come in handy during long matches, tournaments and seasons.

At the end of the day, you can work on these steps over and over again, but if you think too much about the technique rather than just moving to the ball it could be a problem. So just get to the ball as fast as you can, then set a hittable ball. Easy, right? Wink!

SAVING STEPS BY READING THE GAME

Another way to move efficiently is being able to read your own passer's platform. Let's say you're in Rotation 1 in serve-receive behind your outside, standing in right back. Some players are taught to run to the net and then come off the net to set. But if you can read your passer's platform and see that, say, it's outside of their body and their shoulders are up, you can determine that the ball is not going to the net and you can save steps, quickly changing your route. Again, different coaches want different things, but your path to the ball will be much more efficient when you get to a level where you can read the passer's platform.

Being able to read your own passer helps you stay in system even when you're off the net because if you get your feet to the ball, you can run anything. If you're late to the ball, you'll have to bump set or set a high ball or set the back row. You can also judge if the ball is going to the far right side of the court and avoid running to the middle of the net and then having to scramble backward to make the set. This keeps all of your setting options on the table.

How to read the platform is quite simple once you get the hang of it. If the platform is facing directly to you, more than likely it will end up in your vicinity. If the player's platform is facing to the left, it will head in that direction. Same with the right. Lastly if you see the player lift up with a high platform, the ball will likely go up. It takes time to get better at this, and be at a level that you have the time to take in all of these factors. But you will get there, I promise!

Chapter 6

SETTING TOUCH

Your ability to have a good feel for the ball is a very important part of delivering what your hitters need.

A good feel helps you put up solid, hittable balls anywhere on the court, anytime – including on those plays when your feet aren't quite in the right position or your body is a little out of control. A good feel also helps you vary your tempo, setting faster or slower as the situation requires.

The way I developed "feel" was mostly from holding the ball any chance I got. I'd squeeze it, move my hands around it. I had it with me during timeouts and water breaks and warmups. The idea was to continually reinforce the proper hand-positioning and a comfortable feel.

Inexperienced setters often don't have this feel. I see a lot of young athletes setting with their claws – too far underneath the ball, thumbs forward.

Incorrect
Setting with "claws" leads to less accurate sets.

One really important key to setting touch is understanding that your thumbs and wrists need to be back. That's one reason why I teach the "W" hand formation for setting instead of the more traditional "Triangle." I think it gives you more control. When you bring your hands all the way back in a "W," the top of your thumbs will hit your head. In a "Triangle," your thumbs go forward, which can cause your hands to turn and send the ball in a different direction than you want.

Follow through with a Superman flying motion.

The W-shaped hand position is just a personal preference. A lot of very good setters and coaches favor the "Triangle." It's important for you to experiment and figure out what works best for you. I would recommend the "W," but whichever you choose, you need to remember this:

Do NOT follow through with your thumbs! Your follow-through should be like a Superman flying motion, finger tips forward.

GETTING BUY-IN FROM YOUR COACH

The "W" is the way I do it. That doesn't mean it's the only right way to do it, but it works best for me, and I think you should try it – even if your coach has taught you the more common "triangle" technique. You can practice it on your own time and eventually decide which way you prefer.

If you'd like to discuss it with your coach, you can say something like: "I read Lindsey Berg's book on setting, and she thinks the 'W' is the most consistent way to put up a good ball. She teaches it to younger players. What do you think?"

By involving your coach, you make it more of a team effort, which will likely make the coach more receptive to your ideas. Some coaches may not know who I am, but by bringing it up, you give them an opportunity to examine a different approach to setting. Good coaches will view this as an opportunity to expand their knowledge, not a criticism.

TECHNIQUE FOR "W"

I use the "W" hand position because I think it makes my sets more accurate.

Here's how the hand positioning looks for the "W":

The "W" will probably feel strange to you at first. When I teach it, I have players over exaggerate the arm-positioning so their elbows are almost touching. This makes them uncomfortable, but it helps them get the right feel and learn to use their entire body – especially their legs – to deliver the set.

TECHNIQUE FOR "TRIANGLE"

As I mentioned, many coaches teach the "triangle." If you decide this is the best way for you to set, here's how it should look:

"Triangle" hand position is not what I prefer, but you should pick what's best for you.

TWO DRILLS TO IMPROVE TOUCH

Catch and Toss

A great way to refine your touch is to do a series of "catch and toss" reps with a coach or teammate. Here's how it works:

- Hold your hands up with flat wrists and big hands and have your partner toss you the ball.
- Catch the ball and look at your hands. If they look good – nice shape, correct technique – push through the ball with flat palms to target and send it back to your partner.
- Repeat this as many times as it takes to get a good feel. And keep doing this drill until the catch and toss technique becomes second nature. To put yourself in the right mindset, continually think about "ball-shaped hands."
- Be sure to do this drill with back sets as well as front sets. This will help you get confident setting in either direction. This drill can progress to a catch and release, which would be similar to a regular set.

Floor Sets

"Floor Sets" are great for working on your "feel." Here's how they're done:

- Grab a ball and either sit with your legs spread apart or on your knees, whichever is more comfortable for you.
- Push your hands into the ball and push the ball into the ground. Once you have a firm grip on the ball, move it up to your forehead, then release and catch to yourself or a partner. Do as many reps as it takes to establish a nice rhythm.
- A good progression for this drill is to move to a wall and set to yourself. Use the same steps as the previous drill: Push your hands into the ball, push the ball into the floor, move it to your forehead, release against the wall, catch.

This simple setting drill will help you develop a good "feel." Try it with hands shaped in the "W" or the "Triangle," whichever you prefer. Here, I am demonstrating the "Triangle."

- A final progression is moving to the court and setting different targets using the same pre-set routine. The more you get used to feeling the shape of the ball, the easier setting will become in drills, scrimmages or matches.

BENCHMARKS FOR GOOD SETTING TOUCH

The younger you start to refine your setting touch, the better chance you have of being really good at it when you get older. Reps, reps and more reps are the key. As you work on your touch, here are some good ways to gauge your improvement:

- Are you doing reps with all 10 fingers on the ball? I will tell you that I don't set with all 10 fingers on the ball, but when you are developing your technique for doing drills like the ones I've mentioned, you want to have all of your fingers on the ball. If you're setting in a scrimmage or match using "W" hands, which is what I use, you'll probably touch the ball with three or four fingers on each hand. You rarely use your pinkie.
- Are you holding the ball for a long time when practicing? When I teach setters, I encourage them to hold the ball longer while doing reps. For instance, if you are setting off a wall, you'll "catch" the ball (not a full catch; a quick catch), hold it a

little longer, then get the ball out of your hands quickly on your release. By holding the ball a little longer when doing drills, you train yourself to consistently use good touch. As you get more experienced, you can speed up the process.

- Are you practicing setting the ball above your head at every opportunity? When you're not doing drills like the ones mentioned above, you can set the ball above your head repeatedly while walking around – at the gym, at home, anywhere. All you need is a ball. Just set, release and catch.
- Are you following through? The last phase of setting should be a full follow-through with both hands after the ball leaves your fingers. Reach for maximum extension. As I mentioned earlier, your final hand and arm positioning should look like a Superman flying motion with your palms facing outward. This reinforces strong technique, which will lead to more accurate sets.

TRICKS FOR SETTERS

As a setter, especially a shorter setter, you want to have an arsenal of tricks up your sleeve to make yourself that much more valuable to your team. Here are a few that are important to me:

- Holding the ball a little longer but still delivering a legal set. This gives you a better chance to put up a good, hittable ball in tempo.
- Setting in a different direction than your body is moving. Ideally, you want to be squared up to the ball, but in the heat of a match, that isn't always reality. Being able to deliver good balls when things aren't perfectly aligned is key.
- Ability to set off one foot. The game of volleyball is often unpredictable. The ball can be farther away than expected, or it can come directly to your face in a hurry. Having the ability to run and set off of one foot allows you to arrive at the ball quickly and with a more explosive, powerful move. Or, if you're one step off the net and the ball is coming fast at your face, you can take a step with your left foot and set off of the left foot. Both of these skills will improve your game.
- Holding your hands up high so you give the appearance that you are going with a quick set, then being able to adjust to set outside or behind.
- Serving effectively to all six zones. This is actually a good tip for all players, but as a setter, if you are a really good server, it makes you that much more valuable because you will be able to take the other team out of system. So work on your serve – in practice and out.

- Be diverse as a server. Once you've become accurate enough to hit the zones consistently, add some new wrinkles. A jump float. A top spin. Something to mix things up so the other team doesn't know what to expect.

WATCH OTHER PLAYERS

Once I left college and started training with the national team, I began to watch setters from other countries. I took notes when I saw something they were doing that I thought might work for me, then I tried it on my own.

Not everything that works for other setters will work for you, but you won't know if you don't try. And the more you watch, the more you will be able to visualize good techniques and good habits and apply them to your game.

Chapter 7

COMMUNICATING WITH TEAMMATES

If I were writing this book from the most important skill or quality to the least, this chapter on communication would be Chapter 1. I can't express enough the importance of communication with your coaches and teammates. Communication allows you to take charge on the floor, exchange information, lead, encourage and direct. You should work just as hard on becoming better at communication as you do with your setting, serving, defense and all other skills. Good communication improves your entire game just as much as those other skills will.

If you are naturally quiet, I encourage you to step out of your comfort zone. It's very hard to be the best setter you can be without the skill of communication.

KNOWING YOUR TEAMMATES

A big part of establishing a good two-way flow of communication with your teammates is getting to know them off the court and learning what motivates them. The better you know them on a personal level, the more you will understand how to talk to them on the court.

You'll find that different athletes have different needs when it comes to communication. Some are energized by loud, vocal commands. "COME ON! YOU CAN GET THAT BALL!"

Others need to be carefully nurtured and encouraged, so you might be saying things like: "YOU GOT THE NEXT ONE!"

If you want to add a coaching component, you might follow the first statement with something like, "I'LL SET IT HIGHER, AND YOU GO A LITTLE BIT FASTER IN YOUR APPROACH." This instructs the hitter in a positive way, letting her know that it's a team effort and that you BOTH can make adjustments.

Again, some players get fired up by being yelled at, so don't shrink from delivering a loud command if it's necessary and helpful. But keep in mind that some players clearly DON'T like to be yelled at. It's not one size fits all. Your job is to figure out who responds to what and provide it at the right time to get the most out of your team.

If you make a communication misstep by yelling at a teammate who doesn't respond well, fix it at the next timeout. You can apologize or just say something like, "Hey, what I said may have come off wrong. I just want us to play better for the team." Communication like this reduces the chance that the player will go into the tank as a result of what you said, and it will likely help her play with more confidence during the remainder of the match.

BRINGING ENERGY

Along with knowing your teammates, another good way to help your hitters is to exude energy and express confidence in them so they can play more freely and with less fear of making mistakes. When you're covering, you might yell: "I'M RIGHT HERE. SWING AWAY!"

Your energy doesn't always have to be vocal. As a setter, you should be going harder than everybody else to set the standard. Other ways to communicate non-verbally are high fives and taps on the shoulder. Anything to let your hitters know that you are there, you are in control and you are with them mentally on every play, whether it's practice or a match.

TALKING TO YOUR COACH

As the setter, YOU have to be the one to give your coach the unvarnished truth. Setters have a unique perspective that the coach doesn't because they are on the floor and running the offense. If the game plan isn't working, you need to tell your coach that a change is needed. An example would be a plan that calls for setting the pin hitters but the pin hitters aren't producing. You might say to the coach: "Let's try the middle for a while and see if we can change the momentum."

Keep in mind, communication is a two-way street. The coach is going to see things from the sideline that you're not going to see on the floor, whether it's the blockers moving where you can't see them or the other team letting a hitter go.

Another issue is if a player is having a bad day (maybe because of something that happened off the court). You may be more aware of that than the coach because the player is your teammate. So take action! Tell the coach what's up so he or she has a better chance to solve the problem before the match is lost.

If a hitter is struggling during a match, that's another thing you want to talk to your coach about. You might say, "(Name of go-to hitter) isn't the hitter today. Do you have any suggestions on how we can adjust?"

The longer you play and the older you get, the more likely it is that you'll develop a give-and-take relationship with your coach – as long as the coach isn't a my-way-or-the-highway dictator. That happens sometimes, and my message to those coaches is this: Change your ways and be willing to listen to somebody else, particularly your setter. It will make you a better coach because your setter can help you. Working collaboratively is a big asset.

BEING HONEST ABOUT YOUR OWN PERFORMANCE

Maybe you're the one who's struggling. If so, tell your coach. It could be that a certain set isn't working for you. The coach needs to know that. He or she may be able to help.

Establishing good communication with the coach, as I did with Karch Kiraly, is important for all setters.

Remember, it's important that you continue to bring positive energy to the court. Even on a day you're struggling, you have to hold your head high, maintain good body language and continue offering positive feedback to your teammates. If you hang your head and look defeated, you may very well bring the team down with you.

Staying positive doesn't mean you can't acknowledge to your teammates that you're having trouble with certain aspects of your own performance. Part of helping the team maintain good energy is keeping it real, and there's nothing wrong with showing some vulnerability. Ask your teammates for help. You can say something like: "Hey, I'm not setting you the best today. Help me out if you can." That takes a lot of maturity, but it reinforces the theme I've mentioned several times in this book: You and your teammates are in it together.

TAKING BLAME

Setting can be a thankless job. If the hitter gets a kill, the hitter gets the credit. If the hitter doesn't get a kill, the setter often gets blamed.

If you want to be a great floor leader at the setter position, you have to learn to live with not getting much of the credit on good plays and receiving too much of the blame on bad plays. Just don't worry about it. Put up good sets, stay positive, communicate with your teammates and, if needed, do whatever is needed to create a unified atmosphere on the court.

To get the most out of your teammates, it may even be necessary to take the blame even if what happened on the previous play was a hundred percent NOT your fault. Near perfect set and the hitter hits out or gets blocked or hits into the net? You might just say: "I got you. What do you need? Higher? Lower? Do you need it faster? Do you need it more inside?"

To clarify, I'm not saying you should always be saying, "My bad!" If hitters know you are always going to put everything on yourself, it won't mean much to them. What I'm talking about is being encouraging in a way that doesn't leave hitters thinking it's all their fault. "Hey, you got the next one. I'll pull you farther off next time." Or if they are struggling in a game, you can go up to them and say, "Is there anything I can do to help?" This is another way of letting teammates know that you are in it with them.

Once the match is over, you need to handle the outcome much like a coach. Take blame for losses, dish out credit when you win. It's not about you. It's about finding the best way to help your team win.

Chapter 8

JUMP SETTING

Jump setting is an important skill for setters but also a difficult one, so don't rush into it. Your first priority as a young setter should be to get really comfortable setting on the ground.

Inexperienced players often struggle with jump setting because the timing is tricky. This gets better through reps, experience and added physical strength, but before you begin experimenting, make sure you are solid on your hand technique and your follow through.

There's no right or wrong age to start working on a jump set. I started between the ages of 10 and 12. It comes down to comfort level and the strength of your core skill set using your hands. But as your overall skill level increases and you play on higher level teams, jump setting is essential, so you will eventually want to add it to your repertoire. It can be especially useful for setters in faster offenses because it makes it easier to set the middles, and it also helps you establish good, consistent tempo. It's tougher to get good tempo when you're only setting from the ground.

Once you begin practicing a jump set, keep it simple. Try just one or two sets and progress gradually. You probably want to start with pin sets to the outside.

Later in your career, you should be able to jump set everywhere – outside, middle, back. But this may be a two-year process. Or more. If you add too many sets too soon, none of them will be very good.

THREE TYPES OF JUMP SETS

Jump set off two feet.

There are many techniques that work for jump setting. I'm going to teach you the way I do it for both the two-foot jump set and the one-foot jump set.

Jump Set Off Two Feet

Unless you're trying to save a ball that's going over the net, you're not full jumping when you jump set. It's more of a medium jump that establishes your rhythm and forces the blocker to watch you when you're in the front row.

Jump Set Off One Foot

The one-foot set is more advanced. It's more dynamic and gets you to the ball quicker, but it takes a while to get the feel of it.

I liked the one-foot jump set so much that I started using it pretty much all the time later in my career.

Jump set off one foot.

One-Handed Set

The one-hander is an emergency set for saving balls that are about to go over the net. It's very important for shorter setters because they're not able to get up as high on high passes.

The key to producing a hittable set from a ball that is tight and hard to get is keeping it simple. Just tap the ball up a little bit so your middle can get a swing. Don't try to set outside with one hand. That's an extremely advanced skill and not one that should be tried unless you're at the highest level of the game.

Be careful not to contact a ball that's over the net. Refs call that a lot these days, and it's a free point for the other team.

BE PATIENT

Jump setting isn't an easy skill, so don't get discouraged when you first start working on it. It's going to be uncomfortable for a while. Like with all skills in volleyball, you need to work through the rough spots until they feel right. It's worth the effort. You'll be that much more valuable to your team if you're good at jump setting.

Chapter 9

DUMPING

When Toshi Yoshida was head coach of the USA team, he instructed me and our other setter, Robyn Ah Mow, to NEVER dump unless it was absolutely necessary. This directive was given mostly because of our height. At 5-7, Robyn is an inch shorter than I am, and I'm barely 5-8.

Do I agree with Toshi? For the international level of the game, yes. We were competing against the top teams in the world. Stats show that setters our height have less success dumping at that level than they do setting their hitters. That's true at the highest level of D1 college volleyball too.

The juniors' level of the game is different. If you develop good vision that allows you to notice where there are holes in the defense (especially in the middle of the court), dumping can be a huge offensive weapon. Vision is key. You have to learn to see where your opponents are positioned. Is the "donut" open? Are the deep corners empty? Is the left-side blocker bunched in so the back dump is open, or has she dropped off the net into Zone 4 to a spot where she can easily cover the back dump? Look, learn and react.

FRONT ROW DUMP

One of the keys to success with the front-row dump is to make it look exactly how it would look if you were setting. Both hands should be up in a standard setting position when you jump. Some setters actually jump a little lower when they're going to dump to disguise it. A strong jump sometimes tips off the other team.

The contact is just a tap with your left hand to get the ball over quickly to the "donut." Make sure the ball isn't too high. If it's loopy, it's easy to dig.

1 2 3

Success with the front row dump depends on your ability to make the defense think you're going to set.

Two other good locations to place the dump besides the middle of the court are:

1. Deep corners: If the defense is pinched in closer to the middle of the court, the "donut" may not be a good option. Two alternative spots that are hard to defend are deep in the corners of Zone 1 or Zone 5. It takes a certain base level of strength to do this, but if you're physically able, it's a good play.
2. Behind the left-side blocker: On a perfect pass, the left-side blocker will likely be bunched in and standing directly in front of you. This is a good time to back dump behind her. The back dump is also a good choice if the middle blocker has just served because the middle won't be in position to make a play on the ball. Remember, though, if it's not a perfect pass and you get pulled to the left side of the court, the back dump probably won't work because the left-side blocker will have dropped off and will be in the area where you're dumping.

BACK ROW DUMP

I never dumped when I was in the back row. Never! And I don't advise setters who I'm coaching to do it either. I'm not a fan of this play at all! I just don't think it's a better option than setting your hitters.

But like I said before, volleyball is about experimenting to figure out what works best for you, and back row dumps do work for some setters. So you may decide you want to include an occasional back row dump in your repertoire.

First, you should know the rule: If the ball is completely over the plane of the net, it's illegal for a back row setter to dump just as it would be illegal for a back row player to attack.

The technique looks like this:

1 2 3

I'm not a fan of the back row dump, but it may work for you.

Face the four position as if you're going to set outside or back, then shoot over your right shoulder into the donut. Or, if the middle is playing defense in left back, you can shoot back in that area; middles aren't always great at defense, and a lot of times they won't be ready for that ball.

YOUR JOB IS TO SET

There's one more point I want to make. Dumping can be an effective weapon at certain times, but your main job as the setter is to set your hitters. Don't overuse the dump! Your hitters are there for a reason. Give them a good ball and let them do their jobs!

Chapter 10

FITNESS FOR THE JOB

Honestly, my main fitness training for volleyball when I was younger was just playing the game. I know now that fitness training is important for injury prevention and improving your quickness and explosiveness, but most of what I did to stay in shape as a kid was just compete on the beach in Hawaii.

As a teenager, I had the good fortune to play tournaments with older players who had already made a name for themselves – like Lisa Strand Ma'a, who was on the pro tour, and Kisi Haine, daughter of the legendary Tom "Daddy" Haine. I also played with my uncle, Chris Crabb, the father of Taylor and Trevor Crabb, who are now ripping it up on the AVP Tour.

I can tell you with certainty that beach doubles was great for both my game and for my fitness level.

I got stronger, quicker and in better shape from training and competing in the sand, and it also helped my overall game because I had to perform every skill and deal with elements (like the wind) that you don't deal with inside a gym.

UPPER BODY STRENGTH

Arms and shoulder strength are obviously very important for a setter. One thing I would do to strengthen my upper body was set against a wall. I'd go for 10-12 minutes at a time, which made me stronger and also improved my touch.

Practicing setting with a medicine ball can strengthen your technique.

As I got older, I would do these same reps but with a heavier ball – either a medicine ball or a heavy volleyball. I wouldn't recommend this for players below the age of 14 because it takes a certain base strength to set a heavy ball without risking injury. But as you get further into your club and high school years, I think this is highly beneficial.

Another exercise I did regularly was just the standard pushup. This may be old-school, but it's still a popular exercise among a lot of strength trainers for building the upper body. Be sure to use good form. Lower yourself to the floor with your body in a straight plank position, not with your butt pointed up or sagging. The straighter your body, the more benefit you'll get and the less chance you'll have of getting injured.

CORE STRENGTH

A strong core is important for all volleyball players but particularly setters. Your core is what guides all of your body stability. Core strength allows you to set balls from any spot on the court and deliver long-distance sets with good location when you're out of system.

I'm a big believer in planks. They're great for core strength, and you can do them anywhere, anytime. I do several different kinds of planks, which I will demonstrate here.

Standard Planks

Like I mentioned with pushups, proper form is important. Your body should be straight, not piked or sagging.

Standard plank technique.

Side Planks

Side planks are also good core-strengtheners, and they add a balance component. Like with regular planks, you want to make sure your body is straight. Don't bend at the hips.

Side plank technique.

Swiss Ball Planks

Another good plank variation is to use a Swiss ball. Put your arms on the ball the way I'm demonstrating here. You can have somebody move the ball around while you hold your plank steady. You can also do circles or a front-back motion with your arms. All of this strengthens your core for added stability. I did a lot of these late in my career and found them very helpful.

Swiss Ball plank technique.

LOWER BODY STRENGTH AND FOOT SPEED

I also did plenty of agility ladders. This is a good way to warm up, and they prepare you for all of the directional changes you'll make during practices or matches.

Quick sprints are also good. Some players lean toward longer runs for fitness, but if you're a setter, it's all about training yourself for quick bursts. You accomplish this by doing sprints, not 30-minute runs.

KNOW YOUR BODY

Fitness is personal, so you shouldn't think that your workout has to be the same as your teammate's. Consult a trainer and decide on the best way for you to strengthen your body for volleyball.

WARM UP, COOL DOWN

And don't forget to warm up and cool down. Very important. Before you play, do a little jogging, a little shuffling, maybe some body-weight squats. Some players use mini bands wrapped around their legs to activate their lower-body muscles. Band exercises for the upper body are good too.

Recovery after practices or matches is equally important. If you have any specific injuries, you should be spending time with a trainer or physical therapist and maybe getting some massage therapy.

Even without professional help, you can do things on your own to help with recovery. Foam rolling, stretching, icing body parts or even taking an ice bath.

When I was a kid, my teammates and I didn't pay enough attention to warming up, cooling down and recovery. As I progressed in my career, I realized how much better I played when I was diligent about my before and after routines. It's easy to blow them off. Don't! Making time for them will help you feel better, play better and it will lower your susceptibility to injury.

Chapter 11

STAYING ON THE EDGES OF THE GROCERY STORE

I've had numerous conversations with teammates over the years about nutrition. Just about all of them have a similar take. They say they wish they had paid a lot more attention to it in college or when they were juniors.

I feel the same. I trained hard, played hard, did everything I could to be a great volleyball player. But I didn't eat the part until well into my professional career.

My advice to you is to start young – or right away if you are no longer "young." Proper nutrition correlates closely with optimal performance.

One of my favorite sayings on the subject is, "Stay on the edges of the grocery store." This means that you should be eating the clean, real food found on the outer edges of the store, not the processed foods from the inside aisles.

KNOW YOUR BODY

Different athletes have different needs when it comes to nutrition. You may have a teammate who can eat five pieces of pizza with no problem whereas it might cause you to gain weight and/or feel sluggish. I'm not saying that eating five pieces of pizza is a great idea for any athlete. I'm just pointing out that you may react a lot differently to a meal or snack than one of your teammates, so don't base your diet plan on what you see working for somebody else.

CHOOSE THE RIGHT FUEL

Before I talk specifics, let me first say that I am NOT a nutritionist. It's always a good idea to consult someone who is professionally trained when you're making decisions about your eating habits.

With that said, here are some of my nutrition recommendations:

- Include in your meals a lean source of protein (chicken breast, salmon, egg whites, beans) and a healthy carbohydrate (quinoa, brown rice). I remember back in the day when we would "carb load" before matches with a big plate of spaghetti.

Not a great idea! If you do want pasta, control your portions and go with something that's not full of refined flour. Two good alternatives are whole-wheat pasta and chickpea pasta.

There were plenty of healthy food options for the athletes at the Olympics.

- Eat as many veggies as you want. You really can't overdo it with vegetables. But be sure to make them colorful. The more color, the more nutrients. And make sure there are plenty of greens. Kale, broccoli and spinach are great choices. It doesn't matter if they're raw or cooked, just as long as they're not deep fried.
- Choose oatmeal for breakfast instead of pancakes or French toast. Heavy carbs like pancakes can be a real energy suck.
- Stay away from added sugar. If you need sugar, get it naturally through fresh fruit. There's really nothing good to say about added sugar, but natural sugar can, in moderation, be a good source of energy.

- Make your own smoothies. This is usually healthier than buying them because a lot of smoothie places add sugar.
- Don't count calories. Within reason, if you're eating good calories and good fats (avocados and nuts, for instance), you're giving yourself good fuel. Obsessing about each and every calorie isn't a good idea, and it can be a potential gateway to eating disorders.
- Get some food in your system shortly after you finish practices, workouts or matches. Your body needs recovery fuel, so it's important not to let a lot of time go by before you eat.

HYDRATE

You should have a bottle of water with you throughout your day. This is a good habit for anybody, but particularly for athletes. Hydrating on a regular basis helps you perform better and is a key part of the recovery process after you exercise.

DON'T OVEREMPHASIZE BODY FAT

When I played for Toshi Yoshida, he required me to get down to a certain body fat. During that period of time, I didn't play my best and I was also unhappy a lot of the time.

I'm not saying that body fat is insignificant. My point is just that it shouldn't be your primary benchmark when it comes to what you eat and how much you eat. Certain athletes are going to have a little more body fat than others, and that's OK. They may simply have a metabolism that functions better with slightly more fat.

BE PREPARED

Many young athletes don't plan ahead when it comes to meals and snacks. They get up, go to school, go to practice – and then fit in food on the fly.

It's much better if you decide ahead of time the type of food and the quantity that you'll need to match your day's activities. On a day you have practice, matches or fitness training, you're going to need more fuel than a day when you're not exercising.

Don't rely on fast food, vending machines or the tournament snack bar. Bring something from home. This guarantees that you will put something healthy in your body, and it helps you avoid the stress of rushing around to find food in between activities.

Chapter 12

BELIEVE

After 11 chapters that will assist you in becoming the best that you can be, now it's time to believe. When they say you can't, then you HAVE TO!

It starts with believing in yourself. There will be moments that are so tough that you will want to give up. There will be times when you hear the words of doubters. There will be days when you make so many mistakes you won't know how to get out of it.

But I promise you, as Hall of Fame basketball coach John Wooden once said, "If you're not making mistakes, then you're not doing anything. I'm positive that a doer makes mistakes."

The rewards that will come from challenging yourself are priceless. Not only will the process of taking on new challenges, making mistakes and making progress benefit you on the volleyball court, it will also help you in the game of life. The lessons and skills that you will develop will transfer to so many more things.

It never gets easier, you just get better. I promise!

With heart,

Lindsey

About the Author

Lindsey Berg was one of the great setters in the history of USA volleyball, but she didn't fit the prototype. She was told throughout her career by coach after coach that she wasn't tall enough, wasn't lean enough, wasn't good enough.

Turns out, none of that was even close to being true. The 5-foot-8 native of Honolulu played at powerhouse Punahou High in Hawaii, then the University of Minnesota and went on to represent the U.S. in three Olympics. She was co-captain of the 2008 team, which won a silver medal in Beijing, and captain of the 2012 team, which won a silver medal in London.

A big key to Berg's success is that she pushed back whenever someone doubted her. Never was she more motivated than after she got cut from a USA juniors team in high school and noticed that both setters who made the roster were over 6-feet.

"From that point on," she says, "I was on a mission to prove the volleyball world wrong – to prove that it's not necessary to be tall, slim and jump high to be the best in the world."

She did just that, and she tells you how in this book. "The Short Setter's Handbook" is filled with insights into what it takes mentally, physically and technically to reach your potential if you're one of those setters who doesn't look like a setter is supposed to look.